ADDRESS

DELIVERED BEFORE THE

Literary Societies

OF THE

UNIVERSITY OF VIRGINIA,

ON THE

28TH JUNE, 1855,

BY M. F. MAURY, Lieut. U. S. N.

RICHMOND:
H. K. ELLYSON'S STEAM PRESSES, MAIN STREET,
1855.

CORRESPONDENCE.

UNIVERSITY OF VIRGINIA,
June 28th, 1855.

Lieut. M. F. Maury:

Dear Sir—In accordance with a very pleasing duty imposed upon us, we have to tender you the thanks of our respective societies for the very able manner in which you responded to their invitation to address them on the 28th instant, and to request a copy for publication.

With the hope that there may be no interposing considerations to prevent your compliance, we remain, with sentiments of the highest regard,

Your ob't servants,

A. M. SMITH,
J. O. REYNOLDS,
J. A. QUARLES,
Committee of Washington Society.

W. M. FISHBACK,
B. C. BOULDIN,
A. W. COCKRELL,
Committee of Jefferson Society.

UNIVERSITY OF VIRGINIA,
29th June, '55.

Gentlemen:

I have had the honor to receive your note of the 28th inst. It gives me pleasure to comply with the request therein contained, and I therefore enclose a copy of the address.

Respectfully, &c.

M. F. MAURY,
Lieut. U. S. N.

Messrs. A. M. Smith,
W. M. Fishback, et. al.
Committee, &c.

ADDRESS.

The ceremonies and festivities of the occasion which calls us together, mark a period in the career of the student, and give date to an era in his life as a man. The young graduate is now about to take a position in society of great dignity—the independent doer of his deeds ; and to realize a day-dream of his boyhood, by finding himself at last completely and fully invested with the prerogatives and duties of fresh, vigorous, glorious, young manhood.

The responsibilities of a freeman, and the obligations of a citizen in a land where the people rule, are looming up before you, gentlemen.

How to meet and how to discharge them is now the problem for the graduating class.

The demonstration is life-long, and in the mode and manner of it, your name as it is to be remembered when you are gone, is involved; for, as one after another you are withdrawn from the stage of life, the marks that you may leave upon its checkered board, the figures you may have made upon it, will stand in the place of the lettered Q. E. D. which you have been in the habit of writing in these halls, to tell how truly and well you have worked out other problems and finished your task.

Your heritage is in a goodly land. Its fields are wide; its skies are bright; and its people free. Choose you out its men of mark—the great and good—as patterns for yourselves. Ask of their experience, if in its silent teachings you may not find reason—nay more—encouragement, to hope for a good name too—a place among them.

Their spirit answering in the name of both quick and dead, assures us that every son of the soil, how humble soever his parentage, may rightfully aspire to this great honor. Every young man has room for hope here. The institutions of the country guaranty it, and the good spirit that strives with man has planted it in the breast of all who know how to be free.

An American youth setting forth to try the world, commences his career with rare advantages: he has no prejudices of class to overcome; there, the way is clear. Nor has he any superiors save those who have won their claims to superiority by their own industry, intelligence and virtue. It is a race in which no one has any special privilege, but in which all the competitors are equals, everything fair, and the stakes the highest prize that each one may have the spirit or the resolution to contend for.

The young freeman, therefore, who has been well trained, who is possessed of a sound mind in a healthy body, has the chances of a glorious career before him. And well may those, who, long years ago, passed through their training, and are about to finish their course, pause as they approach the goal, to look back and contemplate the scene presented by those who with young blood in blue veins are just setting out. These have great advantages of their predecessors. We are wiser than our fathers: every generation adds to the stock of human knowledge; and however the case may be with individuals, yet with the species there is no doubt that man, generation by generation, grows wiser and wiser. In the discovery of every new truth there is increase of knowledge; and every fresh fact that is revealed to us concerning the mysteries of the universe or the economy of nature, is a clue leading from the very chambers of knowledge, which the discoverer leaves behind him to guide his followers. It is never lost; it marks the spot up to which he had arrived, and his experience serves us instead of knowledge; for we may at pleasure take up the thread and commence where he ended, lead where it may.

Therefore, gentlemen, because knowledge is progressive; because you are young and fresh in the race upon this sea of life; because you have the experience of your fathers, with all the fresh lights and beacons of their knowledge to guide and to warn you, you have great advantages; and because they are decidedly great, the hopes and expectations of friends run high.

When a young seaman is first made the master of a ship, and is about to set out upon a voyage which he has never tried before, it is the practice for him to seek some old mariner who has been that way, and to ask him for sailing directions. These are considered to be the more valuable because they are fresh and directly from experience; and they are heeded the more closely because they "are asked for." There are some here who though not seamen, are nevertheless about to become the masters of their own acts, and who are about to try the voyage of life upon a troubled sea. I have been some little time on that voyage; and it is so, that whenever I see a young man relying upon his own resources, and setting out alone upon this long voyage, my heart warms towards him. I always desire to range up along side of him, to speak to him kindly, and whisper words of encouragement in his ear.

If I give way to the impulse now, and unasked, volunteer a few short sailing directions, I hope you will not take them unkindly.

Every young man in this country has to pass through an ordeal more or less trying or severe, before he can attain a position of influence, or win the privilege of making himself a useful member of the community. Sooner or later the battle of life has to be fought by all; and he who looks aloft and aims high, who has the heart to resolve firmly, the spirit to push forward, and the courage to hope the best,—'tis wise and brave to hope the best—commences this battle with the victory already half won.

There is a trait displayed in this struggle by every American that is very striking. It comes from a principle which when properly cultivated makes men of us all. It seems to be in the air: Our youth breathe it when they are young; and when they are grown, they act up to it unconsciously, for it comes upon them so quietly, and grows upon them so insensibly, that it becomes a part of their nature, and they perceive it not. The source and origin of it are in those great truths which lie at the foundation of our institutions, and have made this nation and people what they are. It is the spirit of progress, the genius of improvement; these impress a peculiar feature upon the character of the true American, and as he pursues his happiness in his own way, they present him in contrast with all the people of the old world.

Take a lad of the people there and catechize him as to his aspirations, and you will find that the height of his ambition is to fill the place and occupy the position of his father. Such is the rule; to do more is the exception. But where is the youth in this country, or the man with the spirit of an American in his breast, that does not look to do better? The more humble the origin, so much the more intensely glows the aspiration. Here the working man—and this is a nation of men who live by the sweat of the brow—must not only have food and shelter; the brute craves that, and the operative abroad has to be content with it—but he strives for the blessings of enough and to spare; he saves that his hands may be strengthened for good, and he accumulates that the field of his usefulness may be enlarged. His desire is to be the kind neighbor, the useful citizen. A man who is not moved by this spirit is under the ban of society here, for with a shake of the head he is called a niggardly or thriftless fellow.

It is this desire to thrive and be useful that carries the citizen into the wilderness. It goes abroad with him in the fields; it comes to him in dreams by night, and in the morning it strengthens him for his task. Operating upon individuals, the masses are moved by its influences to tunnel mountains, level hills, and bridge the mightiest rivers. It has spread a net-work of roads over the land. Its motto is upward and onward; the school-house and the church with its spire pointing aloft, stand side by side for device. Under its guidance this country has flourished and prospered until it has grown to be the happy home of a mighty people.

The right which every one has to pursue his own happiness in his own way; the latitude which he has in the choice of that way, and the free use of faculties and energies that is vouchsafed to him in the exercise of that right, give tone, and vigor, and character to this spirit, making it eminently utilitarian. The proposition it presents to each one is the same, and it is commonly stated by asking a youth what he "intends to be?" thus tacitly admitting the fact, and habitually acting up to the admission, that every young man in this country is the artificer of his own fortune, and may be whatever he has the will and the energy to be.

This being admitted, and having, after careful self-examination, finally selected the avocation most congenial to your taste, perhaps I may, without laying myself liable to the charge of presumption, venture a few hints as to one or two of the objects which every right-minded man, whatever be his occupation, should always keep in view.

The welfare of the community of which he is a member, the prosperity of the commonwealth, are among the objects which the good citizen never loses sight of.

It is, or should be, the duty of every young man to take a newspaper and make himself acquainted, in more or less detail, with the affairs of government, both state and federal. The tendency of a free government with a free press like this, where all great questions are referred to the people and discussed in the primary assemblies, and by the public press, is to make a nation of legislators. Hence the government is always behind the people; it rarely anticipates the press.

In other countries, diplomacy is a profession; but here, every citizen is himself something of a statesman; and it is

2

curious and instructive to compare American state papers with those of any other country. The contrast is both striking and pleasing; and the history of our foreign relations will show that, in all diplomatic correspondence, the strength of the argument, and the force, have generally been on our side.

This is a necessary result of our form of government. Its acts are only the behests of the great popular will. The people are called on, consulted, and appealed to, so often and upon such a diversity of subjects, that the public mind is almost always in a state of more or less excitement with regard to some subject or other, be it federal, state or local. The discussions which take place when the people gather themselves together on these occasions, are full and free; they assume a wide range, and are always instructive. In the excitement thus created, young men of ardent temperaments often get drawn too soon into the vortex of politics: and it not unfrequently happens on such occasions that they are whirled and turned hither and thither to their own great detriment; for such are then but too apt to make politics a trade. This they do in self-defence, for after the lapse of a few years they begin to find that they have neglected their own affairs, and are now without other occupation. How much higher and more noble as to position, is he who, keeping clear of this vortex, has in the meantime been improving his mind and estate, and assisting to advance the prosperity of the commonwealth; who has made two blades of grass to grow where only one stood before; who, besides performing all the duties of the good citizen, has been quietly enlarging his sphere of usefulness, and causing it to spread itself like a circle on the water. It is his rule never to seek office; but have patience: such a man is sure to be appreciated. His fellow-citizens, before he passes the prime of manhood, will be very apt to do homage to his virtues, and to crown him with such honors as a free people only can bestow. Being solicited to take occupation at their hands, he then can judge how best he may serve the state.

In contemplating the history and condition of my own native state, I sometimes am almost persuaded to think it a pity that federal place and honors are so much more alluring in the eyes of many of our young men than anything which the state has to offer. The well-done of this good old commonwealth to her sons is a high honor, and a blessing that the greatest and the best among them have been eager to win and proud to receive. Strive for it: let her have the benefit of your youthful energies, and in the vigor of manhood despise not her benedictions. See what she is; consider what she has been; study her wants and condition, and judge for yourselves as to her true policy.

There was a time when the influence of Virginia among her sister states was paramount. She was their pattern, and they all copied after her. Her sons stood among the foremost in the council of the nation for their manly graces, virtue, and patriotism.

Is it so now? Has she gone back, or stands she where she did; while her sisters improving by the example, have overtaken and passed her in the march of greatness?—by greatness I mean not physical power; I mean moral influence—the power to do good.

Right answers to these questions, gentlemen, are important to you and to her; and it is the duty of the rising generation to discuss them thoroughly and well.

Formerly the virtues of their sons gave states their influence in the councils of the nation, and thence with the other members; now it seems to be votes and numbers.

But since the power of intellect to rule in congress gave way to the force of numbers, the condition of the country has changed; new elements have been brought into play; the material prosperity of all the states has greatly increased, and the relations of business have come up, if not to divide, certainly to modify the power and extent of that kind of influence that Virginia once possessed in so eminent a degree, and which made her in the eyes of all good men so exceedingly beautiful and lovely.

In '98, she had but to speak and her daughter in the great valley of the west would repeat her sentiments.

The polity and code of the Old Dominion then, were code and polity for Kentucky.

But with their iron arms, and the warm embrace of steam, other states have made an impression and won power, weight, and authority there. Louisiana has sent her statutes up the Mississippi by steamboats; and New York, the decisions of her courts of law, by railway. Thus certain features of the Livingston code have been engrafted upon Kentucky jurisprudence on one hand, while on the other, her judges are in the habit of looking to the practice of New York courts for precedents. Through the material agencies of trade has this thing been done.

That the influence of New York with or in the western states has been increasing, while that of Virginia has not been growing, may, I think, be taken for granted. What has brought about this state of things, is one of those questions which, while you are working up to the position of useful citizens, and striving to become influential men in the state, should not, and of course will not, escape your attention. It should be closely examined.

Are the people of Virginia less virtuous and intelligent than formerly they were? I do not think any clue leading to explanation can be found in the answer to this question.

The influence of Virginia, the force of her example, the weight of her authority among her confederates, are not as great as they used to be; or if her influence be as great, that of the other states is not so feeble as it used to be. There is a difference. Is it in the power of her sons to win back the relative weight she once had with them? and if in their power, ought they to recover it for her?

You can never place too much power for good in the hands of the "mother of statesmen." She is virtuous; and the more you strengthen her hands with wholesome influence the wider spreads the circle of her glory; and I take it that there is no son of Virginia here to-day, who does not desire to see the noble old state placed upon the highest eminence that states may reach.

Virginia yields to no state under the sun for the virtue and patriotism of her people. She has done more for this Union than any other member in it; and the time may come—which God forbid!—when her powers to bring into play patriotic and conservative influences will be tried to the utmost.

In recovering or extending her influence, therefore, you will but strengthen her hands for good, and make stronger and more sure the ties which hold the states of this great republic together.

Steam, the telegraph and printing press, have been leveling upwards. There is no intellectual Saul in these days. Commerce is king: therefore, in seeking the power for your state to achieve social conquests by virtuous example, and to hold again the moral sway she once held with her sister states, you should subsidize commerce, and call to your aid all the forces that with a prosperous and thriving people, are seen marshalled in the train of traffic, travel and intercourse. In these lies the secret of the power which every state in a free country may rightfully exercise with her neighbors.

Aim among other achievements therefore, to win for your state that sort of influence which is derived from material agencies; and that kind of moral weight which the opinions that emanate from great commercial centres have with the people at the circumference. London for instance, is such a centre: she through her bankers, and her merchants, and her tradesmen, has put out her commercial tentacles and spread them over the world. They have brought her in intercourse and placed her in contact with all trading people; and, in proportion to the frequency of that intercourse, and the familiarity of that contact, and the benefits resulting from it, is the degree of the influence which she insensibly exercises upon the business, the customs of body, and the habits of mind, in each community. So that now, intercourse, frequent, friendly, commercial and familiar intercourse, is an element in the influence which great states have with each other.

Nearly a hundred years ago, the opinion was expressed by a good thinker who lived here in sight of the Blue Ridge,—a citizen* of the county in which we are,—that the race for power and greatness in America, would be between Virginia and New York, and that it would be decided in favor of that one of the two which should be the first to reach the great valley of the west—then a wilderness—with a commercial portage. New York has accomplished the achievement, and in the act, turned the Mississippi river commercially upside down, for Sandy Hook is almost as great an outlet for the produce of that valley to the sea, as is the South-west Pass at the Balize. But it is yet in the power of Virginia to make the Chesapeake bay, the chief outlet to the Mississippi valley.

Some maintain that it was the *superior* enterprise of the New York people that won for their state this great prize.

I am of the few who question the correctness of that opinion. While the people of New York were confining their energies and their enterprise to her own borders, Virginia was sending out her pioneers and settlers to the "far west," and before the settlements of New York had reached her farthest limits, Virginia courage and energy had laid the corner-stones of two new states in the wilderness.

Again: While New York was planning her works of internal improvement, and striving for the prize which the Virginia seer from his glebe home yonder under the south-west mountains, had pointed out, the mind of the Old Dominion, true to her high calling, was occupied with federal rather than with state affairs. She, in the persons of her sons, was engaged in organizing, arranging, and putting into safe and successful operation this great government, and its free, its noble, its glorious institutions. Washington, Jefferson,

*The Rev. James Maury.

Madison, Marshall, and other master spirits, were engaged upon the great work. They were the principal architects; and like the engineer who plans, lays off and constructs some splendid work of improvement, their whole soul was in their work; it was directed to putting a truly Republican government into successful operation. This done, the magnificent structure, like the railway, the aqueduct, or the bridge, and its subsequent management, may be safely confided to other hands; at least so Virginia appears to have concluded, for federal affairs do certainly engross less of her attention than they did when they were in the hands of her own sons.

A republic with a future of boundless prosperity and inconceivable greatness before it, has been established; its citizens are prosperous and happy at home, honored and respected abroad; and the question as to man's capability of self-government is settled forever.

In this grand achievement, the sons of Virginia bore a noble and conspicuous, may I not say, a chief part? Then may not the mind of the rising generation in Virginia be now turned in right good earnest to the advancement of her own special welfare and glory? In striving to develop the power and resources of your state to her full capacity, many will remind you that you will have to strive against the superior enterprise of the north; but turn the adder's ear to them, and examine the matter for yourselves.

The fairest estimate to be made of the enterprise of a people is based on the average amount of property held by each citizen in the state; for the wealth of the people in the aggregate, is the wealth of the state. According to the statement of Professor Tucker in his admirable papers on the Progress, Population, and Wealth of the United States, which statements are based on the census returns, it appears that in 1850, the average value of the property owned by each white person was, leaving out the cents, $234 per head in New York, against $427 in Virginia. In Pennsylvania the average value of each one's share was

$231; while for Georgia it was no less than $652. I take these states because they are the largest of the old thirteen.

Should we not therefore cast about and seriously think of taking lessons in the study of enterprise, the development of state resources, and the creation of individual wealth, from Georgia, instead of holding up the example of New York and Pennsylvania in a false light, and thus assisting with our voice to give currency to that egregious popular fallacy about the superiority of northern over southern enterprise, as it is called?

I am leading you to a wide field, gentlemen. There is not time to go over it now; if there were, this is not the place, nor am I the person to conduct you through it.

But in seeking to advance the prosperity of your state, you should always take into consideration the climate, as well as the material elements of wealth. The geographical distribution of labor is regulated by natural laws, which we may not with impunity ignore: wherefore, in seeking to foster this or that branch of industry, these laws should be carefully studied. It is they which impress the peculiar traits upon the industrial pursuits of this or that region. Many people in New England, for instance, find it easier to make a living at sea than they do when they attempt to wrest one from the severe climate and stingy soil of their native state; consequently they take to the sea and become sailors. But in the southern states the converse obtains. Here the climate is genial, the soil generous, and the laboring man, instead of being driven away from it to the sea, is invited to stay and dig.

You never hear of a man forsaking his home in the Mississippi valley and going to sea to make a living as a common sailor. But such things are common at Cape Cod. What is the reason? The solution is in those laws of climate and soil which regulate the industrial pursuits of people; and it is in consequence of those laws that we have the absence of sea-faring communities among us;—that the eye of the political economist, when contemplating the industrial landscape presented by Virginia, misses and longs for those very attractive scenes which the business and stir of the sea-calling always impart to it.

That southern youths do not, therefore, like the yankee boys, take to the sea and follow it for a livelihood, is no indication that there is lacking any spirit of enterprise or energy among us. They prefer the land to the sea life. It is in obedience to the laws which regulate the geographical distribution of labor, that one goes and the other tarries; and it was owing to the force of those laws, and not to any superior enterprise, energy, or public spirit, that the business of manufacturing took such deep root at the north, while certain branches of it have always withered or led a sickly existence among us at the south.

That the people of Virginia and the south have not gone as extensively into manufacturing as those of New England have, is no more an indication as to any want of enterprise on our part, than it is want of enterprise on theirs, that the people of New England have not gone as extensively into the cultivation of cotton and rice as Carolina has.

The state of Maine a few years ago attempted to set aside the geographical laws by a decree. Her legislature persuaded themselves that there was a lack of wheat-growing *enterprise* in the state; that instead of depending on other climes for this cereal, it would be better for them to grow it for themselves; and the result was an act giving a bounty to Maine-grown wheat. But it was soon found that one man, by cutting ice from the ponds in winter, and digging potatoes from the ground in summer, could send the results of his labor here to Virginia, exchange them for grain, carry it home with him, and thus, by his own labor in the ice-pond and the potato-patch, put more wheat in the granaries of the state than half a dozen of his neighbors could by laboring in the Maine wheat-field. Of course the bounty act of the legislature could not repeal a physical law; nor did its failure so to do prove the enterprise of Maine to be of no effect. It only showed that the climate and circumstances which regulate the geographical distribution of labor had not been sufficiently studied when the law was passed.

We judge of northern enterprise in a great measure by their works of internal improvement, and by their ventures abroad; yet the first steamship that crossed the ocean was sent over by the south; and the first locomotive that ever blew its whistle in the United States was, I believe, first unthrottled upon southern tracks.

If I were to go into the statistics of internal improvement, I believe they would show that the people of Virginia have also expended more per capitum on works of the kind than the people either of New York or Pennsylvania. Then you may ask, why have not the same results followed?

I answer, for good and sufficient reasons: some are geographical, some political, and some social. Examine for yourselves and you will see them in detail, for I can only glance at them now. The state of Virginia owing to her size and position had, in planning her public works, to consult great diversity of sectional interest. Before she could adopt or establish any policy with regard to internal improvements, her tide-water, her piedmont, and trans-Alleghany sections had to be consulted and conciliated; and in former days, before "commerce was made king," or steam harnessed to navigation, it was not surprising that the people of a tide-water country, abounding with the most choice productions of both sea and land, reticulated with navigable arms and creeks and water-ways leading to the sea, should, to say the least, have been indifferent to any great state work leading over the mountains to that "empire of the west," which was then but little better than a wilderness, but which is now rising up there with such astonishing vigor and rapidity. In New York, the elements for any such marked geographical antagonisms were absent, and in their stead was present a feeling which led to a more judicious location and vigorous prosecution of the works which she undertook. There is at the north too, a more facile spirit of combination and concert by the people, more hearty coöperation between sections than we at the south have been able to boast of; these circumstances, and not the spirit of any superior enterprise, have made the apparent difference between the material prosperity of the states north and the states south.

To meet the emergencies which Virginia considered the most pressing, she produced her Washington, her Madison and her Marshall; she now wants a De Witt Clinton and Jeremiah Thompson. Then she will develop her greatness and make her enterprise palpably as effective as that of New York or any other state can be or ever was.

I don't like those comparisons and stereotyped flings at the south for "*the want of enterprise.*" They are not just. The southern enterprise of this country has done more than the spirit of man has ever before accomplished in the same climates and between the same parallels of latitude; and northern enterprise and southern enterprise taken together, have effected the greatest achievements that human energies have ever accomplished. They have reared the most glorious fabric that the wisdom of sages has ever conceived, and they have set it up here, a light to the whole world, and an asylum to the down-trodden and oppressed of every land. They have developed a degree of material prosperity such as the world never saw and utopians had never dreamed of; and they have made for themselves a home in the wilderness, and surrounded it with all the enjoyments that a free, a virtuous, a cultivated, refined and religious people can crave. Great is the enterprise of the north; not less great is that of the south: they are both glorious.

I said the great works of internal improvement in New York have been more judiciously planned, I should have added, *and executed*; for Virginia also planned a noble work, well calculated to advance her prosperity, to increase her importance, and to enlarge and strengthen her influence with the west through the veins and avenues and arteries of commerce. But she looked back, and now finds herself cut off from that teeming region, and isolated in her position with regard to the trade and travel connected with it. She is suffering from this neglect and failure. An old friend from Nashville, Tennessee, made me a visit in Washington a few days ago. I said, "How did you come?" "By railway through Georgia and South Carolina." "How long did it take you?" "Three days and a half." "Is that the quickest way you could have come?" "No," was the reply, "I could have come a little sooner by way of New York, but there was a day's staging through Kentucky." A bee, if let loose there to come on the wing to his hive, would have passed over an adjoining county in this state.

The geographical position of Virginia is commanding. She is midway the sea coast; nature has made her the front-door to the Mississippi valley—Will you not open it? Her climate is the most healthful, and her harbors the most spacious and convenient in the world; yet even the traveler, let alone the produce and merchandise, must turn aside and pass around her as a *taboo.* Would it not be a good thing for the old state to open her commercial gates as wide as her own hospitable doors, and let all pass through that will?

It would give her influence with the western states and strengthen the ties which hold this union together; for if she can but offer the people there a way to market over which they can fetch and carry on better terms than by other routes, they will straightway become amenable to the influence of her virtue and patriotism, and the time is well-nigh at hand when this union may need it all.

Thus, gentlemen, have we taken a railway sketch of one of the principal fields, and looked over into one or two others among the many rich and fertile ones that are open to you, and in which there is ample room for the display of talents of the first order. Athens was embellished in many ways; and the embellishing of the Old Dominion will always be found to afford subjects of thought worthy of the best minds of the best men in the state.

In entering upon your duties as a citizen, recollect your excellent training here: it has given you many advantages; therefore do not neglect to lay down rules of conduct by which they may be most improved.

Whatever may be the degree of success that I have met with in life, I attribute it in a great measure to the adoption of such rules. One was, never to let the mind be idle for the want of useful occupation, but always to have in reserve subjects of thought or study for the leisure moments, and the quiet hours of the night. When you read a book let it be with the view to special information.

The habits of mind to be thus attained are good, and the information useful.

It is surprising how difficult one who attemps to follow this rule finds it at first to provide himself with subjects for thought, to think of something that he does not know. In our ignorance our horizon is very contracted; mists, clouds and darkness hang upon it, and self fills almost the entire view—around, above and below—to the utmost verge. But as we study the laws of nature, and begin to understand about our own ignorance, we find light breaking through, the horizon expanding, and self getting smaller and smaller. It is like climbing a mountain; every fact or fresh discovery is a step upward with an enlargement of the view, until the unknown and the mysterious become boundless,—self infinitely small; and then the conviction comes upon us with a mighty force, that we know nothing! that human knowledge is only a longing desire.

The impression is very common, that when a young man leaves college he has finished his education; but do not, when you return home crowned with the honors of these schools though you be, give in to this notion even for a moment; it is another of those mischievous popular fallacies that you should guard against. Here you have been disciplining the mind, training the thoughts, and laying off the fields in which they may be usefully employed. You have finished nothing here; you have been only clearing away rubbish and preparing the foundations; and notwithstanding that you have been under the eyes of the best masters, and have laid your foundations of the best materials and in the most scholarly manner, yet like the foundations for any other superstructure, unless built upon they will soon grow weak and be frittered away.

If you stop study now, you will soon forget all you have learned here.

Movement—progress, is a law of the physical world; there, rest and decay are correlative terms. The stars cannot stand still and keep their places; a planet by going back would be hurled into destruction, and even the plant of the earth that ceases to grow, straightway withers and dies. And so it is in the moral world: the progress of man must be upward and onward, or downward and backward. His mind cannot stand still. There is no such thing as a stationary condition for the human understanding. To stand still is death; to go backwards is worse.

With the advantages of the good training which you have received here, you cannot go amiss for subjects of study and improvement. The rock at your feet, the plant in every walk you tread, the air that surrounds you, the insect that flits across your path, the stars that look down upon you, are all suggestive of knowledge. They abound in subjects which it is good for clear heads and sound minds to study and investigate.

When the Spirit of God first moved on the face of the waters, the physical forces that produce the works of nature were brought into play. The wonders, the harmonies and the beauties of creation, are but the display of these forces. As exhibited in the aspects of nature, they are never ceasingly instructive. In the silent hours of the night you may learn excellent lessons from them by watching the "hosts of heaven." I sometimes do this through the telescope; and of all the wonders and beauties that are revealed by this instrument, the simple passage of a star across the meridian is to me the most grand and imposing; it is exquisite! it is lovely! it is sublime! At the dead of night, when the noise of the city is hushed in sleep, and all is still, I sometimes go over alone to the Observatory to revel in this glorious spectacle. The assistants wearied with watching have retired to rest, and there is not a sound to be heard in the building save the dead beat escapement of the clock, telling the footsteps of Time in his ceaseless round. I take up the Ephemeris and find, by calculation made years ago, that a star which I have never seen will, when the hands of that clock points to a certain instant of time, enter the field of the telescope, flit across the meridian and disappear. The instrument is set, and as the moment draws near, the stillness becomes more and more impressive. At last I look—it is glorious! A pure, bright star is marching through the field to the music of the spheres; and at the very instant predicted, even to the fraction of a second, it stalks across the wire and is gone:—The song that was sung by the morning stars has been *felt*, and the heart swelling with emotions too deep for the organs of speech, almost bursts with the unutterable anthem.

The machinery by which the forces of the universe are regulated and controlled is exquisite. And if it be instructive to study the mechanism of a watch, or profitable to understand the principles of the steam engine, the contrivances of man's puny intellect, how much more profitable and instructive must it be to look out upon the broad face of nature and study that machinery which was planned and arranged in the perfection of Wisdom.

If you be at first a little skeptical as to this order and arrangement, taking the harmonies of nature for discord, you will soon feel satisfied that the machinery of the universe—that mechanism which gives nature her powers to act—is in all its parts the expression of one thought,—as much so as the works of a watch are of one design; that the same hand which weighed the earth and gave gravitation its force, adjusted the fibres of the little snow-drop and proportioned their strength. The forces displayed in the blade of grass, in the wing of the bird, and in the flaming path of the comet as it whirls around the sun, are all adjusted with equal nicety and care. Chance has nothing to do with the works of nature; yet there are many of her operations which upon partial investigation only, do look like the results of accident. Botanists tell us of some: They say that certain plants have not the power of scattering their pollen; it is glutinous, and will not fly with wind, but as the insects come to suck the flower, it adheres to them. They lighting on other blossoms deposit it there in the right place for germination. Nay, students of these things go so far as to say that the fig crop of Smyrna, which alone supports thousands of human beings, could not be brought forth if a certain little insect were to fail regularly and at the right time to perform certain offices for this plant. But are not insects as well as plants agents and instruments of the Creator? Have they not their appointed offices to perform in the economy of the universe? And has the insect any more ability to resist the power of instinct than a good seed in good ground has to resist the forces of germination? In studying the works of nature, therefore, discard the idea that they are the result of chance or accident. In the mind of the truth-loving, knowledge-seeking student, the coming of the gall-fly in due season to minister to the fig tree of Smyrna and make it bear fruit for hungry thousands, is no more the work of chance, than it was by chance that the ravens carried bread and flesh in the morning and bread and flesh in the evening, to the prophet at the brook.

www.ingramcontent.com/pod-product-compliance
Lightning Source LLC
LaVergne TN
LVHW011142110826
845150LV00008B/2477
* 9 7 8 1 4 1 8 1 9 2 4 1 9 *